Illustrated Book of

Spirits

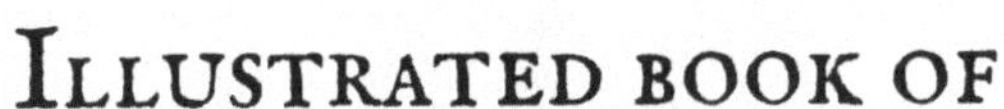

OF THE AIR AND EARTH

DESCRIBED IN
LIBER JURATUS HONORII
ILLUSTRATED BY
SARA KAI GOLDA
PUBLISHED IN 2023

Image of the daemon king Maymon, from Maggs 1929.

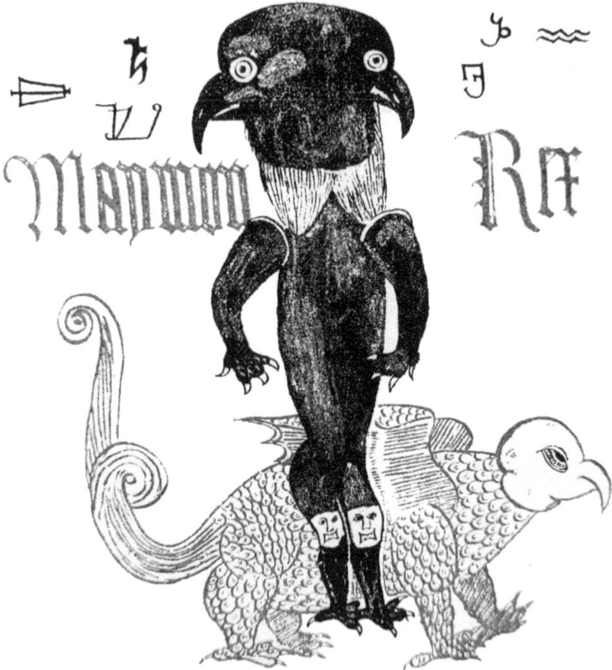

Introduction

The main focus of this book is to portray the spirits described in the Sworn Book of Honorius.
After reading the Sworn Book I haven't found many illustrations of the spirits mentioned. However, I was able to find a clear depiction of King Maymon. This inspired me to illustrate the rest of the spirit Kings. Being passionate about both the arts and the liberal arts, the idea for this illustrated book came naturally. As I have yet to see them, I figured it would be useful to first create them according to my imagination. In my original sketchbook the materials used were watercolor pencils on paper. I tried to be very diligent with their description. I hope this book helps anyone interested with envisioning these spirits and furthering their knowledge on this occult topic.

Sworn Book

The title 'sworn' was chosen to indicate that the reader has sworn to secrecy before ever revealing its contents. It contains a mixture of medieval science and theology. The book was probably influenced by the knowledge from the Jewish Kabbalah, Merkabah and Byzantine texts. The author of the book is Honorius of Thebes, who was most known for creating a magical alphabet. He was a devout Christian, therefore the book incorporates Christian prayers and rituals. Nevertheless, many scholars agree that the book was in fact written by a group of medieval magicians who used this enigmatic name to remain anonymous. Hedegard established that the text was written somewhere between 1100-1350 A.D. The book instructs on the way to obtain a vision of God, create sigils, conjure and invoke spirits.

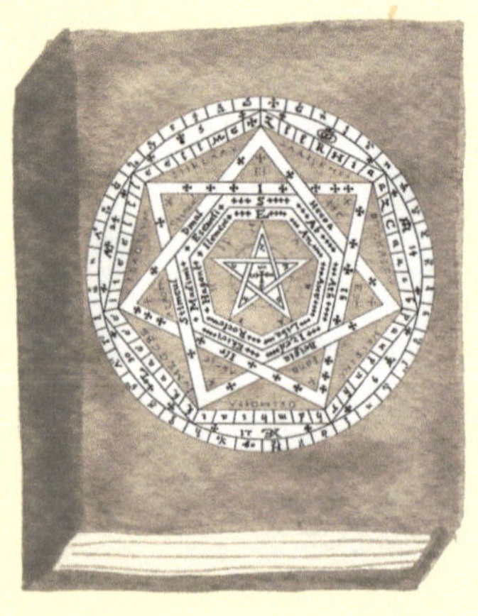

About the Spirits

Each spirit has its own corresponding direction, planet and zodiac sign. According to Honorius some are good, and some are evil. The eastern and western ones are good and helpful, but the northern and southern ones are wild and harmful. This can be seen even in their appearance. Each spirit King has his subordinates, which create an entire system of hierarchy. All of the spirits move differently and each one provokes a different phenomenon when they appear.

The process of invoking the spirits is very meticulous and tedious. It requires a clear-thinking mind and plenty of time dedicated to introspection, meditation and prayer. The process itself involves knowledge of the winds and the use of constraining words. This level of high magic is difficult to master.

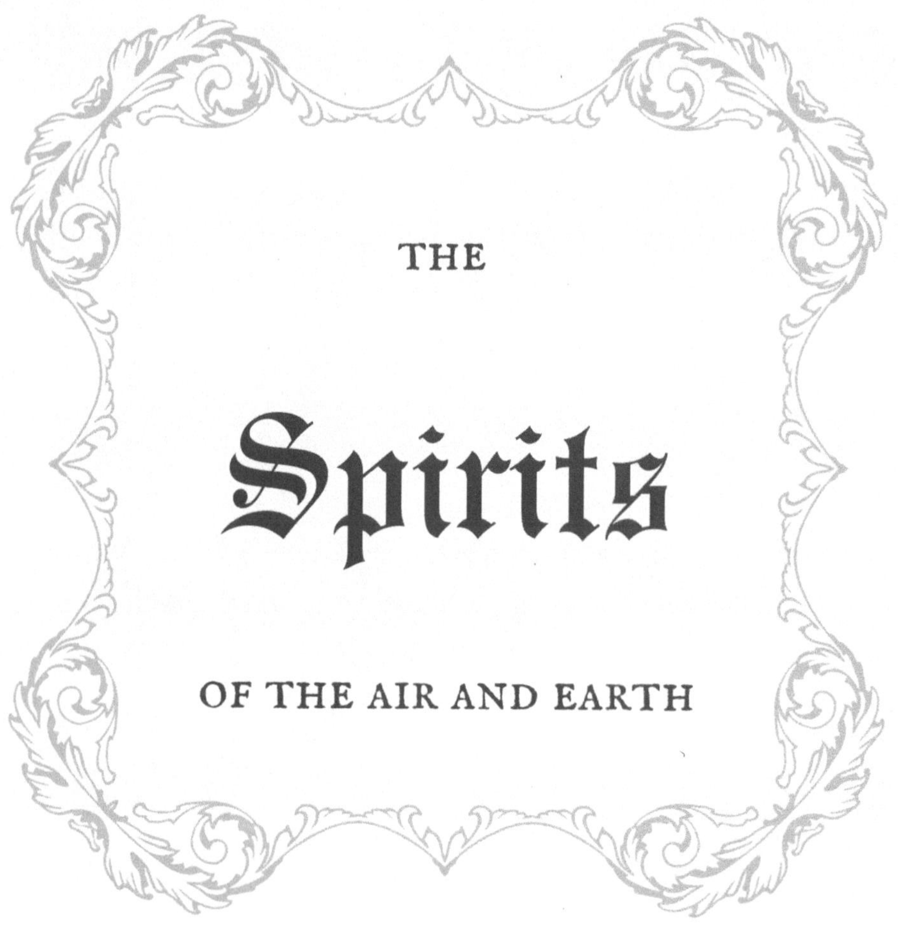

THE

Spirits

OF THE AIR AND EARTH

Spirit Map

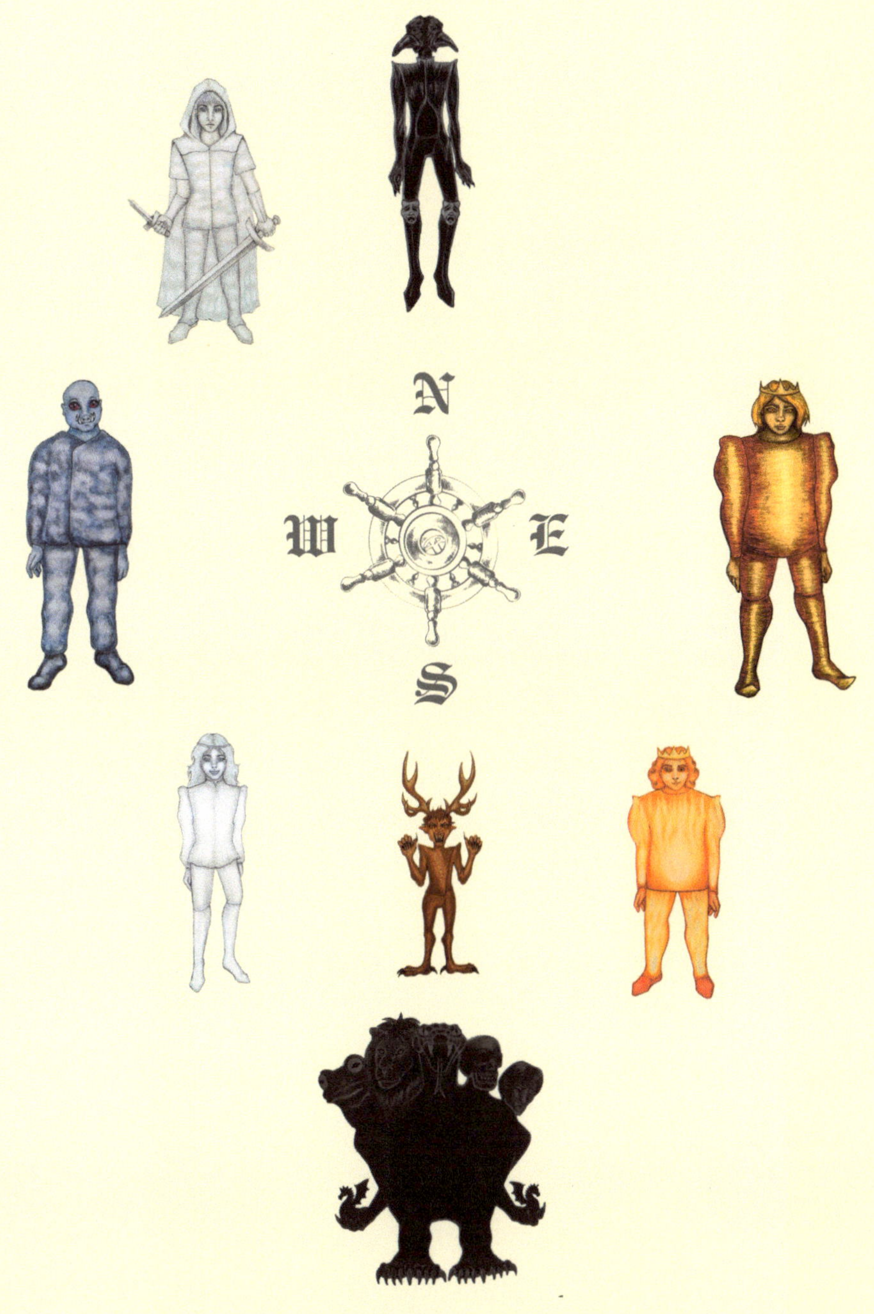

Spirits of the North

They are subordinate to Saturn.

Their King is called Maymon.

They help in evil operations and destruction.

They may cause death.

Their bodies are long, slender and full of wrath.

Their color is shiny black.

Their head has two faces with large and long beaks, measuring three feet. On their knees is another pair of faces, which are in a constant state of sorrow.

They move like the wind.

When invoked an earthquake will be felt and snow will cover the ground.

Zodiac sign correspondence: Capricorn and Aquarius

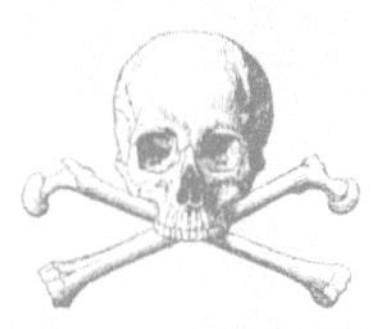

Maymon

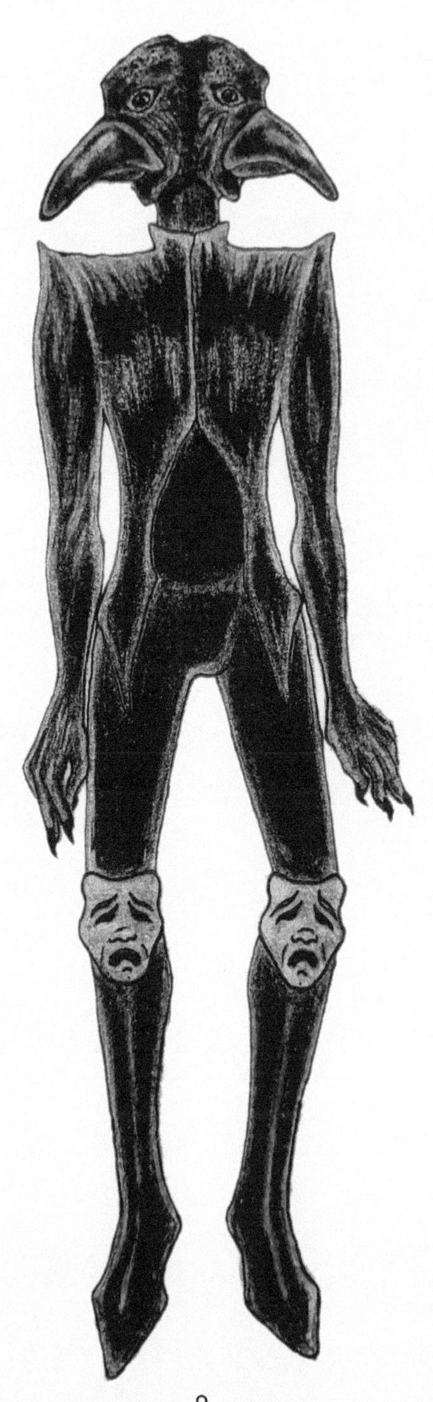

Spirits of the South

They are subordinate to Mars.

Their King is called Iammax.

They grant soldiers.

They help in evil operations, especially in military tactics.

They may excite a war or cause a plague.

Their bodies are small, thin, choleric and ugly.

Their color is like burnt copper.

They have horns like a stag and nails like a griffin.

They howl like mad bulls.

They move like they are burning.

When invoked lightning and thunder will appear.

Zodiac correspondence: Aries and Scorpio

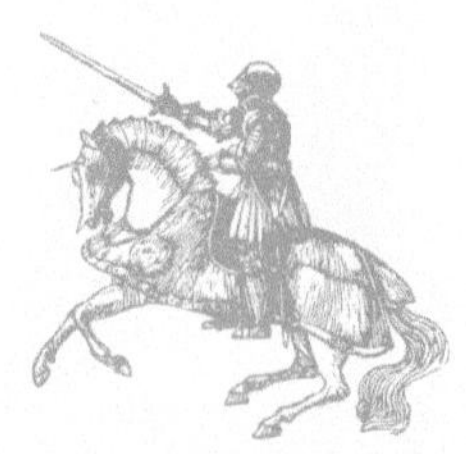

Jammax

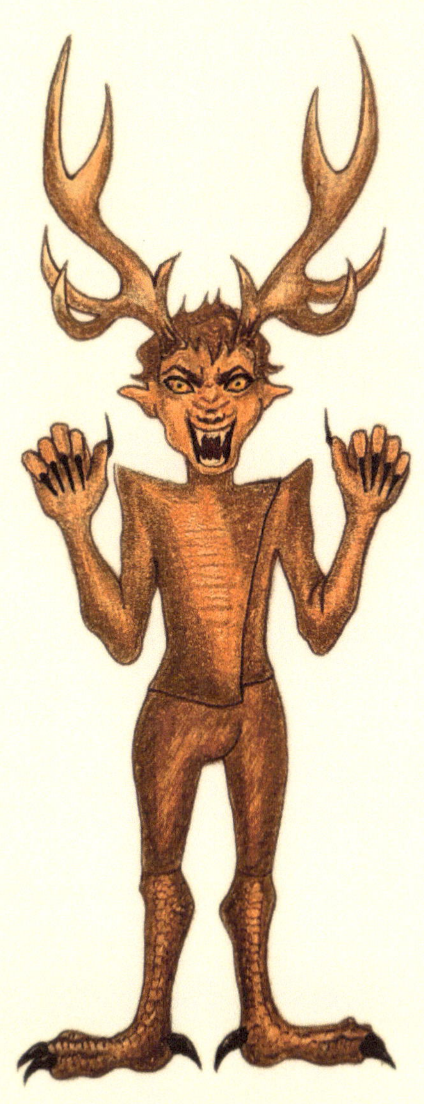

Spirits of the East

They are subordinate to the Sun.

Their King is called Barthan.

They grant gold.

They help in obtaining wealth and honors.

Their bodies are great, large, bloody and thick.

Their color is like polished gold painted with blood.

They move like glitter in the sky.

When invoked the practitioner will break into sweat.

Zodiac sign correspondence: Leo

Barthan

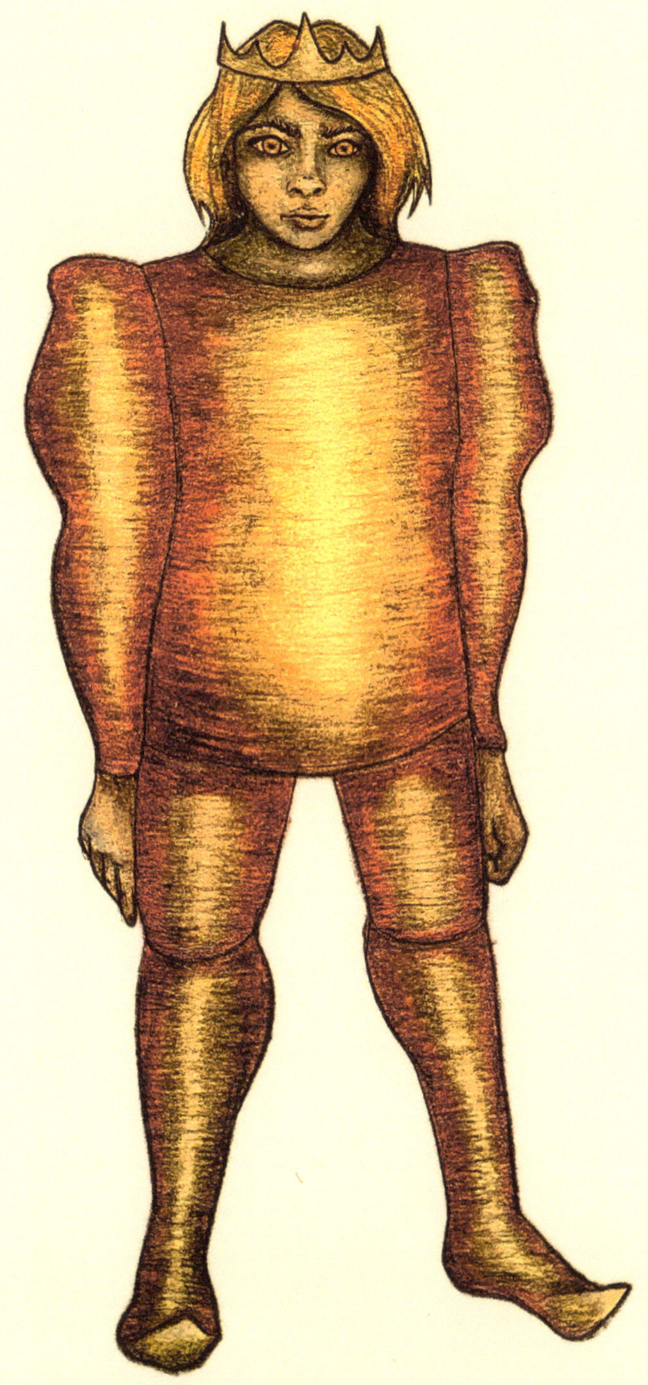

Spirits of the West

They are subordinate to the Moon.

Their King is called Harthan.

They grant silver.

They help in divination and transportation.

Their bodies are large, ample, soft and phlegmatic.

Their color is like a dark cloud.

Their eyes are watery and red.

They are bald and have fangs of a boar.

They move like the sea.

When invoked a great rainfall will appear.

Zodiac correspondence: Cancer

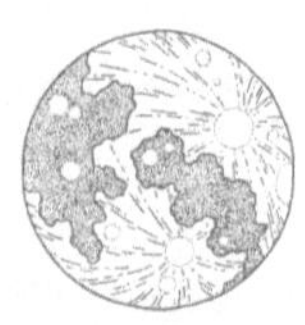

Harthan

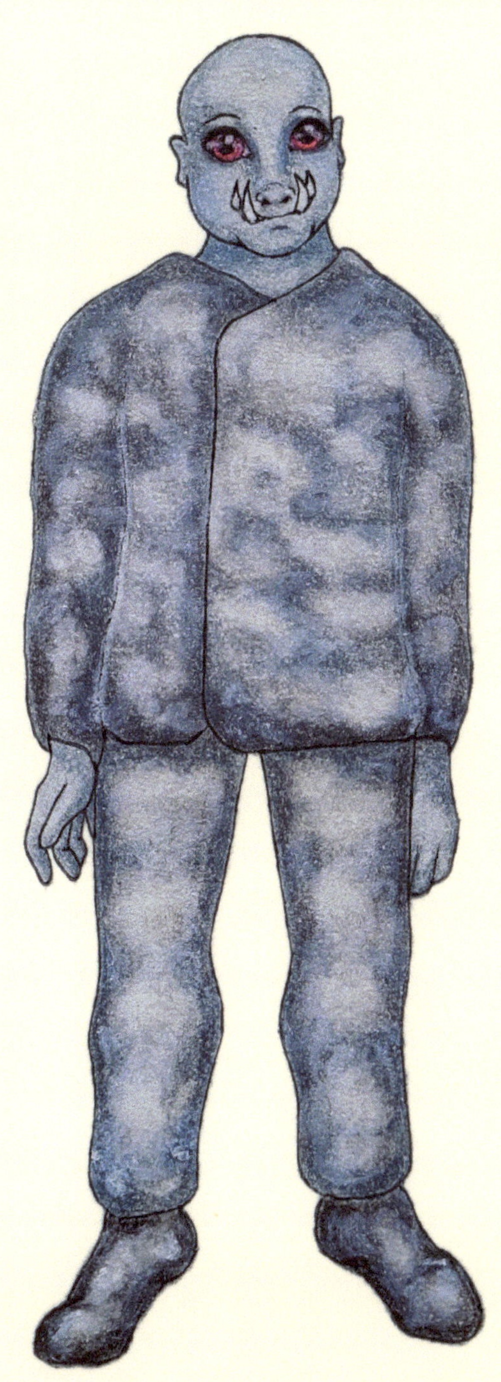

Spirits of the South West

They are subordinate to Venus.

Their King is called Sarabocres.

They grant silver and luxury.

They help in all matters of love.

Their bodies are medium in stature, pretty, pleasant and merry.

Their color is like snow.

They move like a clear star.

When invoked a group of girls playing in a circle will appear.

Zodiac correspondence: Taurus and Libra

Sarabocres

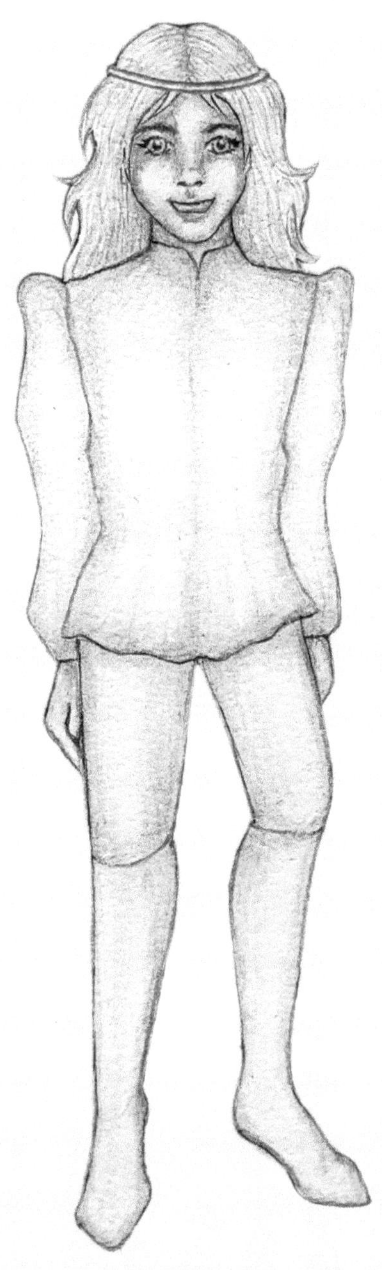

Spirits of the South East

They are subordinate to Jupiter.

Their King is called Formione.

They grant friendships.

They help in healing and bring joy.

Their bodies are large, sanguine and choleric.

They are of medium stature, very jittery and kind in appearance.

Their color is like painted flames of fire.

They move like flashing thunder.

When invoked a lion devouring men will appear.

Zodiac correspondence: Sagittarius and Pisces

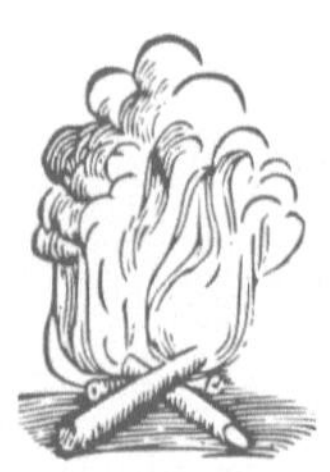

Formione

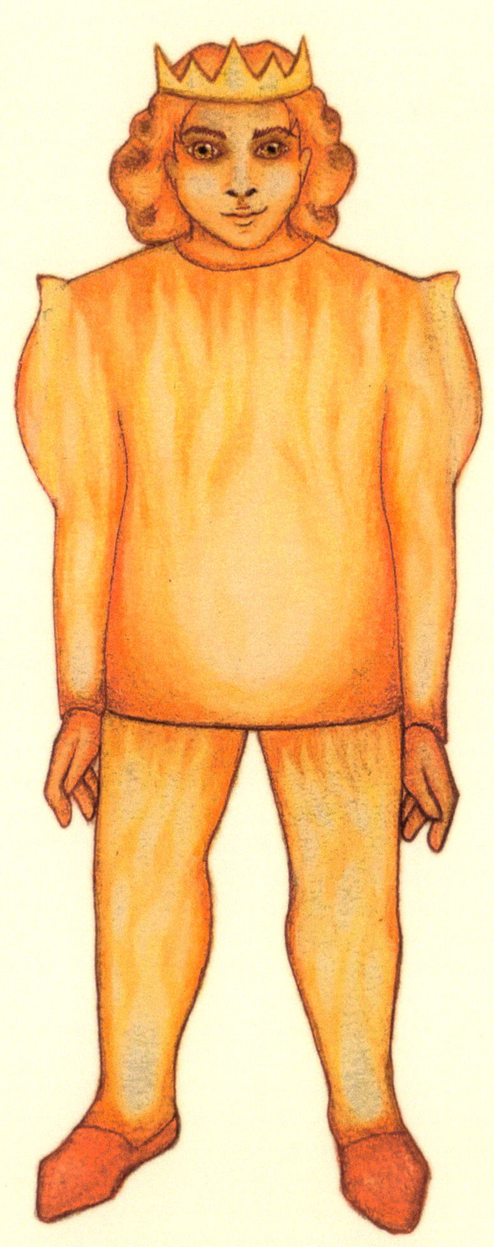

Spirits of the North West

They are subordinate to Mercury.

Their King is called Abaa.

They grant victory and health.

They help in any form of transmutation.

They are very knowledgeable.

Their bodies are of medium stature, cold and attractive.

They have a human form.

They are dressed in a hood and bear arms.

Their color is like a bright cloud.

When invoked the practitioner's hair will bristle.

Zodiac correspondence: Gemini and Virgo

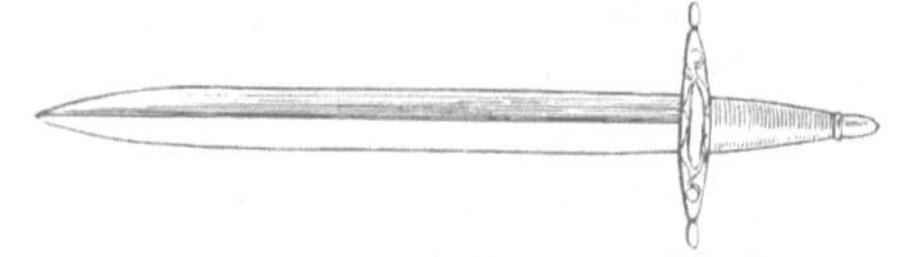

Abaa

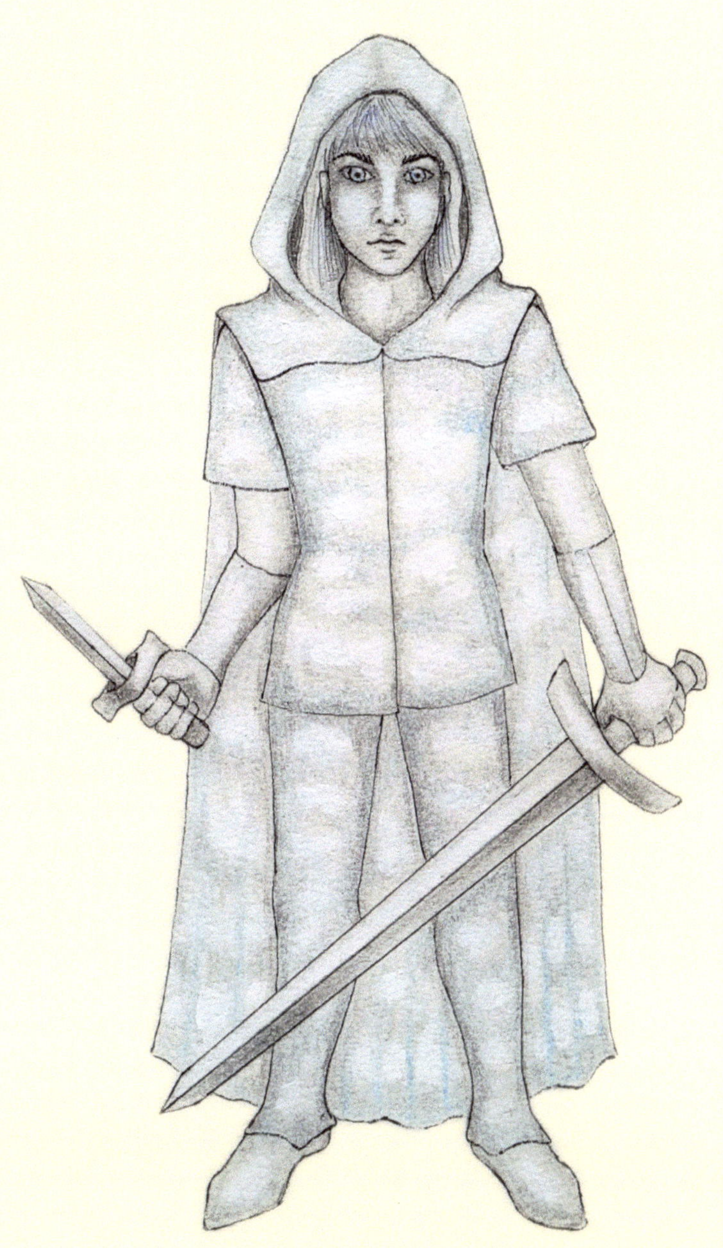

Spirits of the Earth

They are five.
Their southern King is called Corniger.
He has an attendant in all four directions of the world.
Each of the attendants has legions of daemons underneath them.
They are the ministers of hell.
Their prince is called Labadau.
They grant indestructible treasures and precious stones.
They may cause earthquakes and tempt people into destruction.
Their bodies are large, tall and frightening.
Their feet have ten toes and they look like those of reptiles.
They hold two dragons in their claws.
They have five heads: the first is a frog, second a lion, third a serpent, fourth a dead man and fifth a mad man.
Their color is the deepest black imaginable.
Their movement is like that of an earthquake.
When invoked the world will appear destroyed.

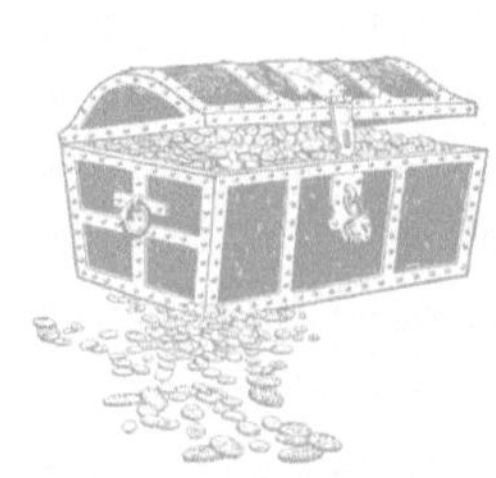

Earth Spirit

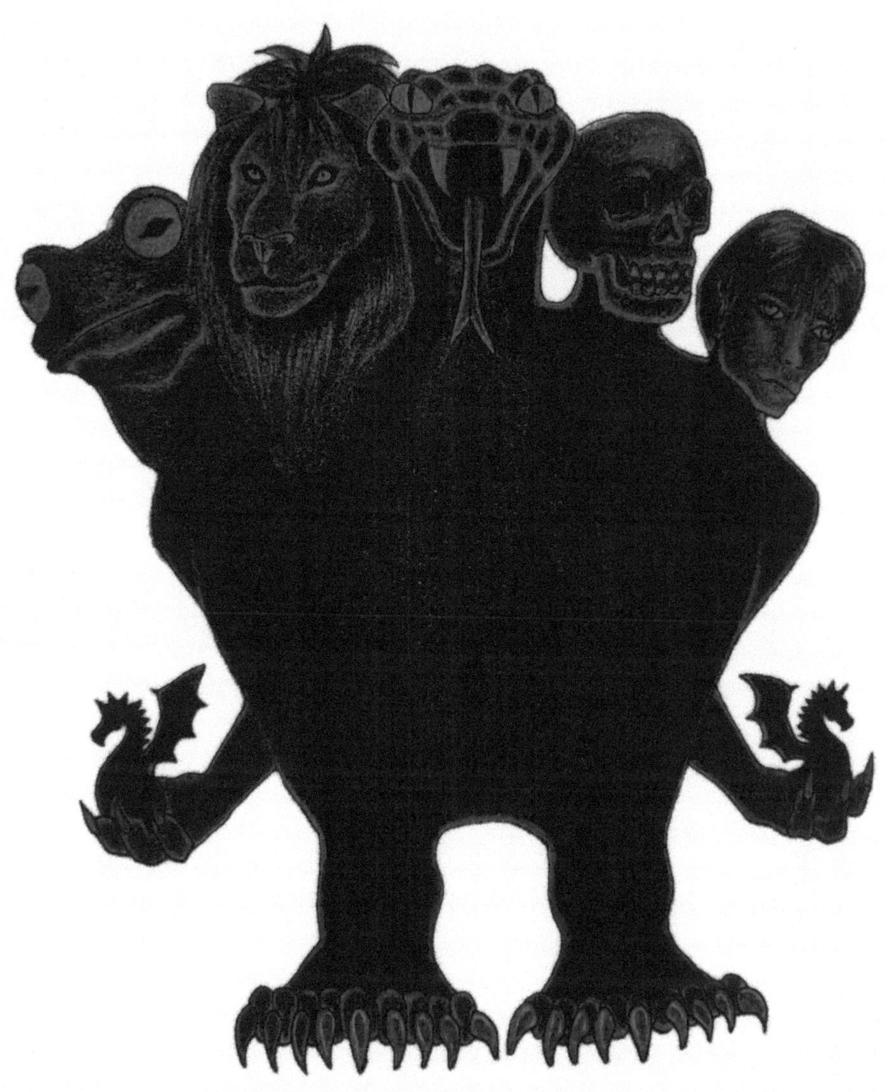

Missing Spirit

It has come to my attention that there is a missing spirit. Honorius never mentioned the spirit of the north east. I will dedicate this paragraph to my speculations. The book clearly states that the spirits correspond to the planets. However, the furthermost planet mentioned is Saturn and his corresponding King Maymon. Therefore, I have come to a conclusion that perhaps the spirit of the north east must be subordinate to either Neptune or Uranus, if of course that spirit if still part of our solar system. If we assume it's one of these planets the spirit would aid in attributes commonly assigned to them, which are innovations or dreams.

If we look at my spirit map we will see that the spirits on the western side are more silver in color and their atmosphere is cold. On the eastern side we see the exact opposite, the spirits not only seem to have a more vibrant disposition, but they also prefer the heat. It is quite probable that the north east spirit will be more favourable towards heat and have the color of something hot, perhaps even ultraviolet. It should be of medium stature similar to the spirits in the opposite angles, like for example Formione. It is difficult to analyse whether it will have any other attributes such as for example Abaa who bears arms. Perhaps it could hold a torch or a staff, a symbol of fire used in tarot. As to the movement it would probably resemble that of heat or light. Nevertheless the north east spirit remains as a mystery...

Spirit Map

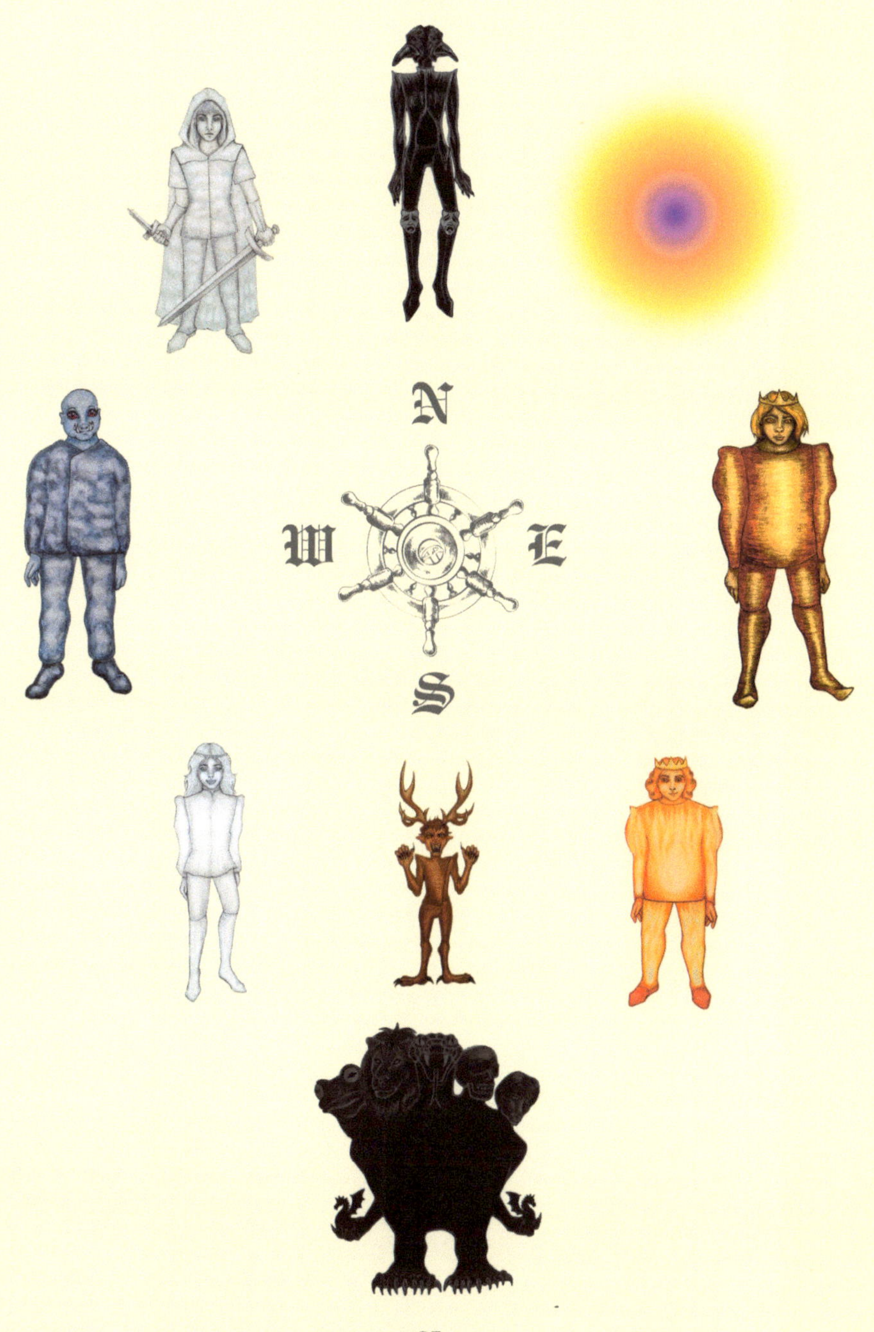

Bibliography

Honorius of Thebes - Liber Juratus

Driscoll, Daniel - The Sworn Book of Honourius the Magician, 1977

Hedegård, Gösta -Liber Iuratus Honorii, 2002

Peterson, Joseph - The Sworn Book of Honorius, 2016

Peterson, Joseph - Elucidation of Necromancy, 2021

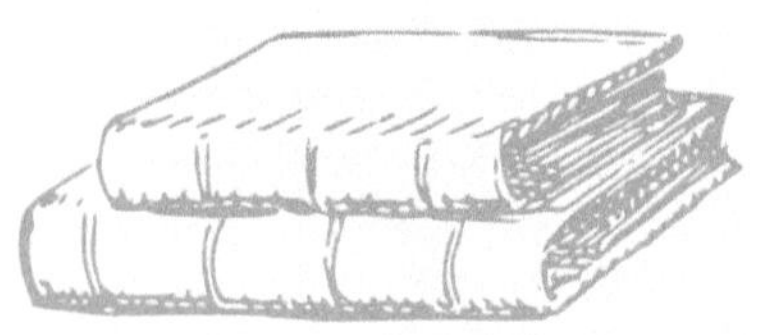

About the author

Sara Kai Golda

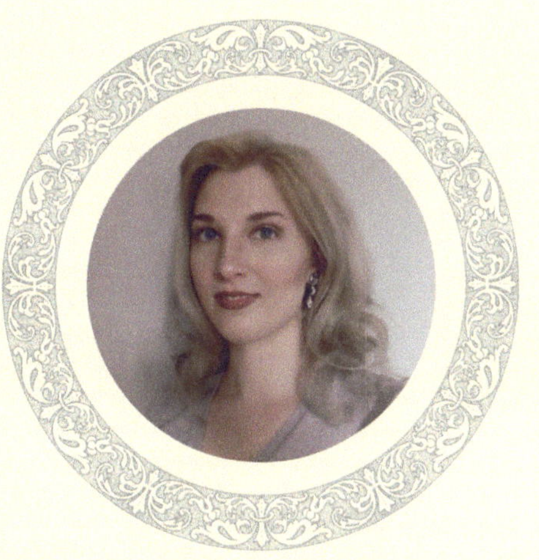

STUDENT OF THE OCCULT
AND LIBERAL ARTS FOR
ALMOST A DECADE.
OBTAINED A DEGREE IN
LAW FROM KINGSTON
UNIVERSITY OF LONDON.
ARTIST.

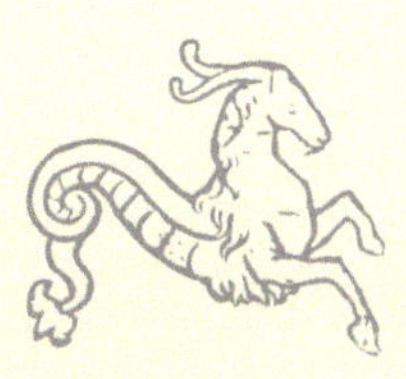

FINIS

www.ingramcontent.com/pod-product-compliance
Lightning Source LLC
Chambersburg PA
CBHW040252240726
48664CB00001B/371